HELEN KELLER

George Sullivan

SCHOLASTIC
REFERENCE

ACKNOWLEDGMENTS

This book might not have been possible were it not for the interest and cooperation of the organizations and agencies that serve persons who are blind, deaf-blind, and deaf. Special thanks are due to Amy Watson, American Foundation for the Blind; Kimberly Emrick, Perkins School for the Blind; Judith Anderson, Alexander Graham Bell Association for the Deaf; Barbara Hausman, Helen Keller National Center for Deaf-Blind Youths and Adults; Sue Pilkilton, Ivy Green, Birthplace of Helen Keller; and Frank Cianflone, Helen Keller Services for the Blind. Special thanks are also due to James Lowe, James Lowe Autographs, for contributing his expertise on Helen Keller's handwriting.

GEORGE SULLIVAN
New York City

LIBRARY OF CONGRESS CATALOGING-IN-PUBLICATION DATA

Sullivan, George, 1927–

Helen Keller / by George Sullivan

p.   cm.—(In their own words)

Includes bibliographical references and index.

Summary: A biography, told using excerpts from her own writings, of the woman who successfully dealt with her own disabilities while trying to better the lives of other deaf and blind people.

1. Keller, Helen, 1880–1968 Juvenile literature.   2. Sullivan, Annie, 1866–1936 Juvenile literature.   3. Blind-deaf women—United States Biography Juvenile literature.   4. Clark, William, 1770–1838 Juvenile literature.   [1. Keller, Helen, 1880–1968. 2. Sullivan, Annie, 1866–1936. 3. Blind. 4. Deaf. 5. Physically handicapped. 6. Women—Biography.]   I. Title.   II. Series: In their own words (Scholastic)

HV1624.K4S85   2000   362.4′1′092—dc21   99-42633   [B]   CIP

ISBN 0-439-14751-4 (pob)

ISBN 0-439-09555-7 (pb)

10 9 8 7 6 5 4 3 2   01   02   03   04

Composition by Brad Walrod

Printed in the U.S.A.   23

First trade printing, January 2001

CONTENTS

INTRODUCTION

"I DO NOT REMEMBER WHEN I FIRST realized that I was different from other people; but I knew it before my teacher came to me. I had noticed that my mother and my friends did not use signs as I did when they wanted anything done, but talked with their mouths."

These are the words of Helen Keller. They are from her book *The Story of My Life*. The book was originally published about a hundred years ago. Helen Keller was a college student at the time.

The story of Helen Keller's life is well known to millions. She lost her sight and hearing when she was less than two years old. With the help

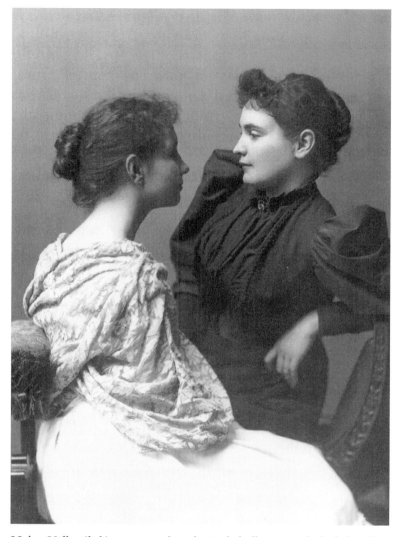

Helen Keller (left) overcame her physical challenges with the help of her teacher Anne Sullivan. For people everywhere, she became a symbol of hope and courage.

of her teacher, Anne Sullivan, she learned to communicate in a world of sight and sound.

Overcoming her physical challenges was not Helen Keller's only goal. She dreamed of a better future for others. She wanted people who are blind "to be able to live naturally and be treated as human beings." Throughout her life, she worked to make that dream come true.

The Story of My Life was the first of nineteen books written by Helen Keller. It is the most popular. It has been published in more than fifty different languages and is available at most libraries and bookstores. Helen Keller also wrote articles for newspapers and magazines.

In *The Story of My Life*, Helen Keller tells exactly what it means to be a person who is deaf-blind.

The actual writing of a book or article was no easy matter for Helen Keller. She would begin by writing what she wanted to say on a braille typewriter. Braille is a system of writing used by people who are blind. In it, raised dots represent letters and numbers.

After she had the braille pages, Helen would copy

them on a regular typewriter. Sighted people could then read what she had written.

But there was a problem. She could not see what she had typed. Her teacher, Anne Sullivan, had to review her writing.

Helen and Anne "talked" to each other by means of the manual alphabet. This is called finger spelling. Through the touch of her fingers into Helen's hand, Anne would communicate letters and words. Helen would answer in the same manner.

People read Helen Keller's books for the amazing stories they tell. They reveal what she was thinking, hoping, and feeling.

In seeking to learn about a person or the past, historians use both primary sources and secondary sources. Primary sources are actual records that have been handed down to us from the past.

There are many different types of primary sources. The Declaration of Independence is a primary source. Abraham Lincoln's Gettysburg Address is a primary source. So is your father's driver's license or a note you wrote to a friend.

Helen Keller "reads" the face of her friend and admirer Eleanor Roosevelt, wife of President Franklin D. Roosevelt.

The Story of My Life and the other books, articles, poems, and speeches actually written by Helen Keller are primary sources. Helen Keller's birth certificate and her college diploma are primary sources, too.

A secondary source is the description of an event by someone who did not witness the event. A secondary source is a second-hand source.

Your history textbook is a secondary source. So is the *World Book* and other encyclopedias. A biography or a magazine article *about* Helen Keller is also a secondary source.

People who lived long ago left many clues about their lives. They wrote letters and kept diaries. They recorded their family trees. They kept business records and took photographs.

Over the years, many of these sources of information are lost or destroyed. When Helen Keller was in her sixties, her home in Connecticut burned down. Many of her important papers were burned to ashes.

But many of Helen Keller's books, letters, speeches, poems, and other such primary sources still exist. They contain important clues. They help us to understand what this remarkable woman was really like.

SUDDEN DARKNESS

"THE BEGINNING OF MY LIFE WAS SIMPLE and much like every other little life," Helen wrote. "I came, I saw, I conquered, as the first baby in the family always does."

Helen Keller was born in Tuscumbia, a village in northwestern Alabama on June 27, 1880. She was the first child of Kate and Arthur Keller.

Helen's father had been a captain in the Confederate army during the Civil War. Afterward, he owned a large plantation on which cotton was grown. He also owned a weekly newspaper.

Mrs. Keller was twenty years younger than her forty-two-year-old husband. She was his second wife. His first wife had died.

Captain Keller had two sons from his earlier marriage. One of Helen's half brothers was named William Simpson. He was a teenager when Helen was born. The other half brother was James, who was in his early twenties.

Helen's mother helped to run the farm. She cooked and she sewed. She grew vegetables and tended the chickens, turkeys, sheep, pigs, and other farm animals.

The Keller house was surrounded by huge trees. It was also covered with ivy. They called the house "Ivy Green."

A smaller house stood close to the main house. It was called "The Little House." It had two

Helen Keller's father, Captain Arthur H. Keller, served with the Confederate Army during the Civil War.

rooms. Helen was born in "The Little House" and lived the first few months of her life there.

As an infant, Helen had soft golden hair and pale blue eyes. She was bright and eager. It was said that at the age of six months she could say "How d'ye" and "tea, tea, tea."

She also knew the meaning of the word

Kate Keller, Helen Keller's mother, had Northern roots. Her father was born in Massachusetts.

"water." She pronounced it "wah-wah." On her first birthday, Helen took her first steps.

These were happy days for the Keller family. But they did not last long.

One February day in 1882, Helen suddenly became ill with a very high fever. She had a bad headache and stiff neck. The doctor called it "fever of the brain and stomach." Some doctors believe that Helen may have had scarlet fever.

For a while, the doctor thought Helen might not live. But after several days, the fever left as suddenly as it had come.

Helen's mother and father were greatly relieved. But they soon became aware that something was terribly wrong. At night, Helen slept poorly, tossing and turning. When her name was called, she did not respond. Her eyes did not close, even when her mother put a hand close to Helen's face or bathed the child.

Helen's mother and father soon realized the awful truth. Their daughter was losing her ability to see and hear.

"I was too young to realize what had happened," Helen would write many years later. "When I awoke and found that all was dark and still, I suppose I thought it was night, and I must have wondered why day was so long coming. Gradually, however, I got used to the silence and darkness that surrounded me and forgot that it had ever been day."

The Kellers' main house, "Ivy Green," as it looks today. The house has four rooms on the first floor, with a fireplace in each room.

Helen now lived in a world of silent darkness. What few words she had learned before her illness, she soon forgot. She would cry when she wanted something or was in pain. She would grunt when something pleased her. But these were the only sounds she made.

Because she could not express herself or understand anyone, Helen was often angry. She became very difficult to live with as a result. Her temper tantrums were frequent. She would sometimes hit, bite, or pinch other people. She later admitted to being a "wild, destructive little animal."

She once pinched her grandmother and chased her from the room. Some relatives looked upon Helen as "a monster." They said she should be sent away to a hospital for the mentally ill. But Helen's mother had no thought of doing that.

Helen wanted people to understand her. So she began using hand signals and other gestures to express herself. She later explained them. "A shake of the head meant 'No' and a nod 'Yes,' a pull meant 'Come' and a push 'Go.' Was it bread that I wanted? Then I would imitate the acts of slicing and buttering them. If I wanted my mother to make ice cream for dinner, I made the sign for working the freezer and shivered, indicating cold."

Helen's father wore glasses. When she wanted to refer to her father, she pretended to be putting on glasses. To suggest her mother, Helen pulled her hair into a knot at the back of her head.

Helen in a rare quiet moment. As a child, she was stubborn and had a quick temper.

By the time she was five years old, Helen had about sixty signs to tell people what she wanted.

She understood a good deal of what was going on in the world around her. She learned how to fold and put away clean clothes, and she could tell her own clothes from the others. Helen knew when her mother dressed to go out. She would tug at her mother's skirt and beg to go with her.

Helen also learned to be a mischief-maker. When she was five, she found out what keys were for. Not long after this discovery, she locked her mother in the pantry. She kept her locked there for three hours. She knew she had done something wrong. She couldn't hear her mother pounding on the door. But she could feel the vibrations of the pounding. She sat outside on the steps and laughed.

Helen never forgot locking her mother in the pantry. Another event that became fixed in her memory was almost tragic.

One day, Helen happened to spill water on her apron. To dry it, she stood in front of the fireplace, holding the apron up to the flames. The apron did not dry fast enough for her. Helen moved closer and closer to the burning logs. Suddenly, the apron burst into flames. Then her clothing caught fire. Helen screamed. Fortunately, Helen's nurse was nearby and heard her screams. She threw a blanket over Helen, snuffing out the flames. Helen escaped with scorched hair and slightly burned fingers.

By that time, Helen knew that she was different from other children. She wrote, "I noticed that my mother and my friends did not use signs as I did when they wanted anything done, but talked with their mouths." Helen did not understand this. She tried moving her lips. But she did not know how to form words. "This made me so angry at times that I kicked and screamed until I was exhausted."

Helen's outbursts of anger became more and more frequent. She would lose her temper several times a day.

When Helen was five, a second child, named Mildred, was born to the Kellers. Helen once found her doll's cradle occupied by her baby sister. "I grew angry," Helen wrote. "I rushed upon the cradle and overturned it, and the baby might have been killed if my mother had not caught her as she fell."

Helen's parents knew that Helen needed help. But there was no school for people who were blind or deaf near where they lived. And it did not seem likely that any teacher would come to Tuscumbia to work with Helen. Her parents did not know what to do.

TEACHER

ONE DAY WHEN HELEN WAS SIX years old, her father took her to visit a doctor in Baltimore. The doctor examined Helen's eyes. Then he told Captain Keller that Helen would never see again.

But the doctor was impressed with Helen. He found her to be a bright and lively child. He told Captain Keller that he believed that Helen could be taught just as other children. The doctor had a suggestion for Captain Keller. He told him to take Helen to Washington, D.C., to see Alexander Graham Bell.

Alexander Graham Bell was very famous. In 1876, when he was twenty-nine, Bell invented the telephone. He was also well-known for his work with those with hearing impairments. He had once operated a school in Boston for teachers of people who had suffered hearing loss.

Captain Keller arranged a meeting with Alexander Graham Bell in Washington, where he was carrying on his work with people who were deaf. Helen and Bell liked each other from the moment that they met.

Helen sat on Bell's lap, and he let her play with his pocket watch. Using her fingers, Helen felt the vibrations as the watch chimed the hour.

"He understood my signs," Helen would later write, "and I knew it and loved him at once." Helen Keller and Alexander Graham Bell would remain friends until Bell's death in 1922.

Bell advised Captain Keller to write to the Perkins Institution for the Blind in Boston. The Perkins Institution had opened in 1831. It was the first school in America for people who are blind. Perhaps they could suggest a teacher for Helen, Bell told Captain Keller.

As soon as he returned home, Captain Keller did

Helen Keller (left) and Alexander Graham Bell remained close friends until Bell's death in 1922. The two are pictured here with Anne Sullivan in 1894.

as Bell suggested and wrote to the Perkins Institution. Not long after, the Kellers received a reply from Michael Anagnos, the school's director. He told the Kellers that he had a teacher in mind for

Helen. She was, said Anagnos, "exceedingly intelligent, strictly honest, industrious, [and] ladylike in her manner." Besides that, she was "familiar...with the methods of teaching deaf, mute, and blind children."

The teacher's name was Anne Sullivan.

Anne Sullivan's parents were immigrants from Ireland. They had settled in western Massachusetts, near Springfield. Anne, the oldest of the five Sullivan children, was born in 1866.

When she was five, Anne developed a serious eye disease. It was not properly treated. She became almost blind as a result.

Anne was ten when she and a younger brother were sent to an institution in Tewksbury, Massachusetts, that provided for people who were needy and disabled. There, life was difficult, even tragic. Her brother became ill and died.

One day officials from the state of Massachusetts visited the institution. Anne flung herself at the group, pleading for a chance to go to school. In

1880, the teenaged Anne became a student at the Perkins Institution for the Blind.

While at Perkins, Anne came to know Laura Bridgman, a woman in her fifties. Laura was the first person to be educated in the United States who was deaf-blind.

To communicate with Laura, students at Perkins would form letters through the touch of their fingers into the palm of her hand. The letters together made up what is called the manual alphabet. The manual alphabet is very similar to the sign language alphabet used by people who are deaf.

Anne Sullivan learned to finger spell using the manual alphabet during her years at Perkins. Doing so enabled her to "speak" with Laura Bridgman and other people who were deaf-blind.

As she got to know Laura, Anne felt sorry for her. Laura spent her days sewing and praying. She had no life outside the school.

In 1886, when she was twenty years old, Anne graduated from Perkins. Her eyes had been operated

Laura Bridgman (with glasses) works with a fellow student at the Perkins Institution for the Blind. Laura Bridgman lost her sight and hearing at age two because of scarlet fever.

on twice while she was attending the school. These operations had greatly improved her eyesight.

Anne was ready to set out on her own. But she had no idea of how she was going to earn a living.

Then Anne heard from Michael Anagnos, the director of the Perkins school. Mr. Anagnos wanted to know if she would like to become a private teacher. Her only pupil would be a girl who was deaf-blind in Tuscumbia, Alabama. Anne had doubts about herself. She didn't know whether she could teach a disabled child. But Mr. Anagnos had faith in her. He said she could do the job if she made up her mind to do it.

Captain Keller then wrote to Anne. He invited her to come to Tuscumbia. He said that the Kellers would pay her twenty-five dollars a month and "treat her as one of the family."

Twenty-five dollars a month seemed like a very good salary to Anne. And she had no other job offers. So in March 1887, Anne set out by train for Tuscumbia. In her suitcase, she carried a doll, a gift for Helen from the students at Perkins.

After a long train trip, Anne finally arrived in Tuscumbia. Mrs. Keller and her stepson, James, were at the station to greet her. Anne and the Kellers got into a horse-drawn carriage for the drive to the

Keller home. As they drove, Anne noticed that Tuscumbia looked like the New England villages she remembered from her childhood days. The dirt roads cut through plowed fields. The fruit trees were in blossom.

As they got closer to the Keller house, Anne became more and more excited. "I could scarcely sit still," she once recalled. "I felt like getting out and pushing the horse faster."

CHAPTER 4

WILD CHILD

HELEN HAD A FEELING THAT something important was going to happen that day. Her mother had spent the morning hurrying about the house. Early in the afternoon, she felt her mother put on her hat and her gloves. That was a signal to Helen that her mother was going somewhere.

Helen wanted to go with her. She tugged at her mother's skirt. But Mrs. Keller gently brushed her aside. Then she went off in the carriage. James went with her.

Helen sat on the steps of the front porch and waited for her mother to return. She didn't know that a stranger was arriving. Helen didn't like strangers. It made no difference to Helen that the stranger was Anne Sullivan, whom the family would call Annie. It didn't matter that Annie was coming all the way from the Perkins Institution in Boston to try to help her.

Late in the afternoon, Helen felt approaching footsteps. It was Annie Sullivan. Helen thought it was her mother. She put out her arms. But it wasn't her mother. It was a stranger.

Helen felt the stranger's arms coil around her. She kicked and twisted and struggled to get away.

Although Helen was fearful of strangers, she was also curious about them. She approached Annie Sullivan again. She suddenly snatched Annie's handbag and began to go through it, searching for candy. When her mother took the handbag away, Helen burst into a rage. She screamed and rolled on the grass.

Annie did not know that this was quite normal behavior for Helen. She did not know that Helen was a wild child. If Helen did not get her way, a tantrum was the result. She would fling herself on the ground and let out ear-piercing screams. Helen's mother did not even try to control her. Helen's tantrum did not discourage Annie. The day after Annie arrived, she began Helen's first lesson. Annie planned to teach Helen to spell, using the finger alphabet that she had learned at the Perkins Institution.

Annie Sullivan in 1887, the year she arrived at the Keller home to begin her long association with Helen.

She took the doll that the children at Perkins had given Annie as a gift for Helen. Annie placed the doll in Helen's hands. Helen liked it; she hugged it.

Then Annie took one of Helen's hands and spelled out the letters D-O-L-L in Helen's palm. Next she took Helen's hand and stroked it lightly over the doll.

Annie then repeated the lesson, first spelling out

the word doll in Helen's palm, then brushing her hand over the doll.

Helen seemed to catch on. She began to imitate what Annie was doing. Slowly, she spelled out the letters D-O-L-L in Annie's hand.

But Helen did not really understand. "I did not know that I was spelling a word or that words even existed," Helen would later recall. "I was simply making my fingers go in monkey-like imitation."

The second word that Annie tried to teach Helen was *cake*. She spelled the word into Helen's hand. Then she gave her a piece of cake. Helen gobbled it down. But she did not understand the connection between the word and the cake itself.

Helen had no idea that Annie was her teacher. She didn't know that Annie was there to instruct her. All she knew was that this stranger was trying to make her do things that she sometimes did not like to do.

One morning at the breakfast table, Helen and Annie clashed bitterly. Family meals at the Keller home were seldom quiet and orderly. Helen was permitted to wander around the table and take whatever she wanted from anyone's plate. But Annie refused to allow Helen to take food from her plate.

When Helen reached for a piece of food, Annie slapped her hand. Helen reached again. Annie slapped her hand again. Helen screamed and burst into a tantrum.

Annie asked Helen's mother and father to leave the room. She locked the door behind them and went back to eat her breakfast.

Helen was still down on the floor, kicking and screaming. She stopped screaming long enough to try to jerk Annie's chair out from under her.

When she was unable to unseat Annie, she got up to find out what was happening. When she realized that Annie was eating, she tried to snatch a piece of food from her plate. Annie slapped her once again. Helen got back at her by pinching Annie's arm.

Annie slapped her hand again. Helen pinched her back. Annie slapped her hand once more. And so it went—slap-pinch-slap-pinch.

Tiring of the game, Helen made her way around the table, touching all the chairs. When she found that they were empty, she seemed puzzled.

She went back to her own chair and sat down. She began eating her breakfast with her fingers. Annie gave her a spoon. Helen threw it on the floor. Annie forced Helen out of her chair, and made her pick up the spoon. When she got Helen back into her chair, Annie made her take the spoon in her hand. After more struggling, Helen finally began to eat her breakfast with the spoon.

There was another quarrel over folding the napkin. When she had finished eating, Helen threw her napkin on the floor and ran for the door. When she found it was locked, she kicked and screamed. Annie led her back to the table and made her sit down. Then Annie presented her with her napkin and made Helen understand that she was to fold it. It took an hour.

When the job was done, Annie opened the door. Helen ran out into the warm sunshine. Annie went to her room. She was worn out. She felt beaten. She threw herself down on her bed and wept.

GREAT STEPS

H ELEN'S FAMILY HAD ALWAYS allowed her to do exactly as she pleased. If she did not want to comb her hair, it remained uncombed. If she did not want to pick up her dolls, they remained scattered about her room.

When Helen's mother or father tried to force her to do something she didn't want to do, Helen would boil with rage. Her habit was to scream and throw herself on the floor.

Helen's mother and father could not stand her tantrums. They decided that life would be easier if they let their daughter do whatever she wanted to do. Her father especially felt this way. He could not bear to see Helen cry.

Soon after Annie Sullivan arrived, she realized

that the Kellers were making a mistake. Helen had to be taught to behave. Otherwise, Annie knew that she would never be able to teach Helen anything. But Annie also realized that she could not control Helen unless she got her away from the family. She spoke to Captain Keller about moving with Helen out of the main house, away from the family.

To Annie's surprise, Captain Keller agreed. He suggested that Helen and Annie move into "The Little House," the two-room house where Helen had been born. It was close to the main house, but it would allow Helen and Annie to be by themselves.

The first few days in "The Little House" were difficult. Helen kicked and screamed when she understood that she had to stay there. When she quieted down, she spent her time playing with her dolls. She would not let Annie touch her.

Helen stayed in a bad temper for several days. She frequently gave the sign for her mother. At the same time, she would shake her head sadly. She played with her dolls more than usual. She would have nothing to do with Annie.

"The Little House," near the Keller family's main house, was where Helen Keller was born.

Several days after Helen and Annie had been living together, the two had an early morning quarrel. Helen would not put on the clothes that Annie had given her to wear. Annie made Helen understand that she would have no breakfast until she got dressed.

Around ten o'clock that morning, Captain Keller happened to look through a window in "The Little House." He was surprised to see that his little girl was still in her nightgown. He was so upset that he decided that he would "send that Yankee girl back to Boston." Later, however, the captain changed his mind.

Little by little, Helen began to change. There were still times that her temper flared, but her outbursts were not so violent.

About two weeks after Helen and Annie had moved into "The Little House," Annie wrote a joyful letter to a friend at the Perkins Institution. "My heart is singing for joy this morning. A miracle has happened!...The wild little creature of two weeks ago has been transformed into a gentle child. She is sitting by me as I write, her face serene and happy, crocheting a long red chain of Scotch wool.

"She lets me kiss her now," Annie's letter continued, "and when she is in a particularly gentle mood, she will sit in my lap for a minute or two...

"The great step—the step that counts—has been taken."

The "great step" would soon lead to an event that some people would call a miracle.

Day after day, Annie spelled words into Helen's hand. Helen would then take Annie's hand and spell each word back. It was like a game to Helen, and she enjoyed it. But she did not link the words to the things they stood for. B-R-E-A-D was just a series of letters to Helen. She did not know that it meant a baked food.

"She has no idea yet," Annie Sullivan wrote, "that everything has a name."

One day, Helen and Annie began their daily spelling lesson. Helen was in a restless mood. She was being difficult that day. Annie decided that they should take a break. They headed for the water pump at the back of the main house.

Helen described what then happened in *The Story of My Life*. "Someone was drawing water and my teacher placed my hand under the spout. As the cool stream gushed over one hand, she spelled into the other the word water, first slowly, then rapidly. I stood still, my whole attention fixed upon the motions of her fingers.

"Suddenly, I felt [as if] somehow the mystery of

The water pump behind the family home in Tuscumbia where Helen discovered the use of language.

language was revealed to me. I knew then that W-A-T-E-R meant the wonderful cool something that was flowing over my hand."

After Helen had spelled out "water" several times, she dropped to her knees and pointed to the ground and asked for its name. She pointed to the pump and asked for its name. Suddenly, she pointed to Annie and asked for her name. Annie slowly spelled out T-E-A-C-H-E-R. From that time on, Annie was "Teacher" to Helen.

Now Helen was eager to learn. "Everything had a name," she wrote, "and each name gave birth to a new thought.

"I learned a great many new words that day," Helen continued. "I do not remember what they all were. But I do know that mother, father, sister, teacher were among them. . . .

"It would have been difficult to find a happier child than I was as I lay in my crib at the close of that eventful day and lived over the joys it had brought me, and for the first time longed for a new day to come."

TO READ,
TO WRITE

AS SOON AS HELEN LEARNED WHAT letters meant and that everything had a name, a new world opened up to her. "I did nothing but explore with my hands and learn the name of every object that I touched," Helen later wrote.

By the summer of 1887, Helen knew more than four hundred words. She quickly learned how to use them to construct simple sentences. These she spelled out in Annie's hand.

To learn about nature, Annie took Helen outdoors for many of her lessons. "Miss Sullivan taught me to find beauty in the fragrant woods, in every blade of grass...," Helen wrote.

Helen learned to tell one flower from another by touching the petals and stems. She touched the leaves and bark of different kinds of trees.

Annie brought Helen to a nest of straw where a chicken was hatching eggs. She let Helen hold an egg in her hand as a baby chick pecked its way out. She also introduced Helen to a squirming baby piglet.

When the circus came to Tuscumbia, Annie was able to acquaint Helen with many animals that were unfamiliar to her. Helen got to feel the ears of a giraffe and shake hands with a trained bear. She hugged a lion cub and rode on an elephant.

Sometimes lessons were held on the banks of the Tennessee River near the Keller home. "I built dams of pebbles, made islands and lakes, and dug river-beds, all for fun, and never dreamed that I was learning a lesson. She [Annie] made raised maps in clay, so that I could feel the mountain ridges and valleys, and follow with my fingers the devious course of rivers."

One summer day in 1887, Annie decided it was

Helen and Jumbo, one of the Keller family pets.

time to teach Helen to read. Annie had gotten several special books from the Perkins Institution. These books had their words printed in raised letters. People who were blind could read these books with their fingertips.

Annie began by first spelling a letter into Helen's palm. Then she pressed Helen's fingertips to a piece of cardboard upon which the raised letter appeared. Annie and Helen went through the alphabet slowly, one letter at a time. In one day, Helen learned the entire raised letter alphabet.

Then Helen learned to use the raised letters to form words. Next, she arranged the words into easy-to-understand sentences.

As soon as Helen was able do that, it was not hard for her to read simple books printed in raised letters. Helen loved to read. She became an eager reader for the rest of her life. She read, she said, "everything in the shape of a printed page that has come within the reach of my fingertips."

That spring Helen also learned how to write. To make letters and words, Helen used a special writing board. It had horizontal grooves about an inch apart. The grooves went from one edge of the board to the other. A sheet of paper was first placed over the board. Then Helen would write letters on the paper, using the board's grooves as a guide.

In shaping the letters, Helen held the pencil in her right hand. She used the index finger of her left hand to help out.

It was hard work for Helen, demanding great effort.

The Story of my Life
Helen Keller.
1902

Cordially yours
Helen Keller.
undated

Helen Keller
1944

Helen Keller
1945

Helen Keller
1949

Helen Keller.
1955

Helen Keller's signature changed little over the years.

She ended a number of the first letters she wrote with the words "I am tired" or "I am too tired to write more."

One of Helen's first letters was addressed to her cousin Anna. It had no commas, periods, or other punctuation marks. It had no capital letters. It read:

helen write anna george will give helen apple simpson will shoot bird jack will give helen stick of candy doctor will give mildred medicine mother will make mildred new dress

Not long after Helen celebrated her seventh birthday, she faced another hard challenge. Annie wanted her to learn braille.

Braille was developed in 1824 by Louis Braille, a French teacher of people who were blind. People with visual impairments are able to read braille by running their fingertips over raised dots.

Helen was delighted by braille. She much preferred producing words by braille to writing with pencil on paper. With braille, she could read whatever she wrote.

A	∶∶	F	∶∶	J	∶∶		N	∶∶		R	∶∶	V	∶∶
B	∶∶	G	∶∶	K	∶∶		O	∶∶		S	∶∶	W	∶∶
C	∶∶	H	∶∶	L	∶∶		P	∶∶		T	∶∶	X	∶∶
D	∶∶	I	∶∶	M	∶∶		Q	∶∶		U	∶∶	Y	∶∶
E	∶∶											Z	∶∶

0	1	2	3	4	5	6	7	8	9
∶∶	∶∶	∶∶	∶∶	∶∶	∶∶	∶∶	∶∶	∶∶	∶∶

Raised dots on paper (here represented by black dots) stand for letters and numbers in the braille system of writing.

As soon as Helen had become skilled in reading braille, Annie introduced her to braille books.

By now, Helen's tantrums had ended. Her thirst to learn continued to increase.

Christmas that year was the happiest holiday the Kellers could remember. For the first time, Helen took an active part in the celebration. She and Annie prepared surprises for everyone.

Helen was thrilled to find presents in the stocking she had hung. And there were also gifts for her on the table, at the door, and on all the chairs. "I will write many letters," she tapped into Annie's hand, "and I will thank Santa Claus very much."

TRIPS NORTH

LATE IN 1887, HELEN WROTE A LETTER to the "dear little blind girls" at the Perkins Institution. In the letter she promised to come and visit them.

The next year, not long before her eighth birthday, Helen kept her promise. Annie and Helen's mother took her north to Boston, Massachusetts.

On the long train trip, Annie sat next to the window. She tapped out a steady stream of words into Helen's palm, describing what she saw. They passed the Tennessee River, hills and woods, and cotton fields that stretched as far as the eye could see.

When they arrived at Perkins, Helen was

thrilled to meet the school's children. She was delighted to find that they could "talk on fingers." The children told her about their lives at Perkins. She joined them in their games.

Helen felt at home at the school. "I was in my own country," she wrote.

In the Perkins library, Helen found the largest collection of braille books in the United States. Helen pounced upon the books, sending her fingers skimming over the raised-dot pages.

Of books, Helen wrote: "They tell me so much that is interesting about things I cannot see. And they are never troubled or tired like people."

When the Perkins Institution closed for the summer, Annie and Helen visited the seashore at Cape Cod. Helen had always lived far from the ocean, but she had read about it. As a result, she longed "to touch the mighty sea and feel its roar."

The sea did not disappoint her. The breaking waves, she wrote, "filled me with exquisite, quivering joy." After her first dip, she wanted to know, "Who put the salt in the water?"

Helen (standing at the left) with other students at the Perkins Institution for the Blind.

By now, Helen was beginning to become famous. Stories were appearing in the newspapers about the amazing child who was deaf-blind and could understand words and read. One newspaper called her "the wonder girl." To another, she was "a miracle."

Michael Anagnos, the director of the Perkins school, praised Helen at every opportunity. He called her a "marvel."

Helen and Annie were now able to communicate with each other at amazing speed. Helen could spell into Annie's hand at the rate of eighty words per minute. Annie was the only teacher able to keep up with her.

But Helen was not satisfied. She was not happy talking only with her fingers. She wanted something more. She wanted to be able to speak with her lips. She asked Annie to teach her to do so.

Annie didn't like the idea. She felt that Helen might fail which would make her sad.

But Helen insisted. Finally, when Helen was nine years old, Annie took her back to Boston. There, at the Horace Mann School, Sarah Fuller, the school's principal, began to teach Helen to say words.

Teaching a child who is deaf-blind to speak is no easy matter. It takes special skills. For a hearing

Helen, at thirteen, was already world famous.

child, learning to speak depends on listening to speech. The child repeats what he or she hears. A child who is deaf uses his or her sight and sense of touch to learn to speak.

But with a child who is deaf-blind it is very different. It is much more difficult. The child has only a sense of touch to rely upon.

Helen described how Sarah Fuller tried to teach

her. "She passed my hand lightly over her face, and let me feel the position of her tongue and lips when she made a sound. I was eager to imitate every motion and in an hour had learned six elements of speech: M, P, A, S, T, I."

The lessons continued. Helen was thrilled when she was able to utter her first sentence: "I am warm."

But the words were poorly formed. Only Sarah Fuller and Annie could understand from Helen's deep grunts what she was trying to say.

Vocal cords produce a person's voice. But Helen's vocal cords were very weak because she had never spoken. She could not produce clear sounds.

Helen realized this. In a letter to a friend in Boston, she wrote, "Oh, Carrie, how I should like to speak like other people! I should be willing to work night and day if it could only be accomplished. Think of what a joy it would be to all my friends to hear me speak naturally."

To help improve her voice, Helen entered the Wright-Humason Oral School in New York City.

Annie was always at her side. Helen's classmates were mostly students who were deaf. The speech lessons did not produce the results that Helen hoped for. She never learned to speak clearly. Most people could not understand her unless she spoke very slowly. She also had to use simple words.

"I suppose we aimed too high," she wrote.

Besides working on her ability to speak, Helen was also taught to read lips. She did this by feeling the movement of the speaker's lips and throat. The speaker had to speak slowly. Each word had to be pronounced carefully.

Helen's ability to read lips and speak had an important benefit. She got to know even more about the world around her.

Helen also studied arithmetic, geography, French, and German at the Wright-Humason school. Geography and German were her favorite subjects. Arithmetic bored her.

Helen and her classmates went on many field trips

Helen reads Annie Sullivan's lips with her fingertips.

in New York City. They visited the Statue of Liberty and Central Park. They went to museums and the theater. They even went to a dog show.

Helen and Annie made many new friends in New York City. These included John D. Rockefeller and Andrew Carnegie, two of the richest and most famous business leaders of the time.

Helen also met Mark Twain, the well-known author. Helen had read and loved *Huckleberry Finn* and many other of Twain's books. The two became close friends.

When she met Twain, she ran her fingers through his hair and over his face. She put some violets she had been given into the buttonhole of his coat. She kissed him on the cheek when he said good-bye.

Twain came to look upon Helen as the most remarkable woman he had ever met. He once heard a man feeling sorry for Helen because of the "dullness" of her life. Twain was quick to correct that idea. "Blindness is an exciting business, I tell you," Twain declared. "If you don't believe it, get up some dark night on the wrong side of the bed when the house is on fire and try to find the door."

COLLEGE DAYS

ELEN WAS STILL ATTENDING THE Wright-Humason school in New York when she received the news that her father had died. Helen was heartbroken.

But her father's death made Helen think. She began to realize that she could no longer depend on others. She had to learn to be independent.

She made up her mind to prepare herself for the years ahead by going to college. But she wanted to go to a "regular" college. She wanted to go to a college where the students could see and hear.

Helen's choice was Radcliffe College, a women's college that was part of Harvard University. (Harvard closed Radcliffe in 1999.)

Attending Radcliffe seemed like an impossible dream. In the 1890s, few women were educated beyond high school. College was mostly for rich men.

To be accepted by Radcliffe, Helen had to pass the college's entrance test. To prepare for the test, Helen entered the Cambridge School for Young Ladies in Boston.

Helen was now sixteen years old. This was the first time she had lived among girls her own age that could see and hear. "I took long walks with them," Helen wrote later. "We discussed our studies and read aloud the things that interested us. Some of the girls learned to speak to me, so that Miss Sullivan did not have to repeat their conversation."

After six months at the Cambridge School, Helen's sister Mildred joined her as a student. "We were hardly ever apart," Helen recalled.

Helen spent two years at Cambridge. After completing her studies there, she took the entrance test for Radcliffe. She passed and entered Radcliffe in the fall of 1900. She was the first student who was deaf-blind to ever attend an American college.

Helen sought to be treated the same as all of the other students. She attended regular classes. She typed her papers on a regular typewriter. She took swimming lessons and gym. She went on class picnics.

Mildred Keller, Helen's sister, joined her as a student at the Cambridge School for Young Ladies.

The only difference was that Helen had Annie at her side much of the time. Annie described to Helen every room they entered. She told Helen what her teachers and the students looked like and how they were dressed.

Books in braille or raised letters were few. Each book that Helen was assigned to read had to be finger spelled—letter by letter—into Helen's palm.

Annie Sullivan reads to Helen by finger spelling each word into Helen's hand.

Annie also spelled into Helen's hand all that was said in classroom lectures. When the teacher spoke rapidly, it was a problem. Annie sometimes found it impossible to spell out every word.

After each class, Helen would rush back to her room. There, she would set down in braille what she could recall. She astonished Annie by all that she was able to remember.

Annie would spend four or five hours a day reading and spelling into Helen's hand. The burden upon Annie gave her headaches. It also caused her eyesight to fail. At times, Helen had to stop attending class to give Annie a chance to rest her eyes.

Aside from Annie, Helen had few friends at college. Only one of her classmates knew how to finger-spell. When a fellow student tried to be friendly and spoke to Helen, Annie would have to spell the words into her hand. This made it difficult to make new friends.

To show their friendly feeling toward Helen, her classmates bought her a dog, a Boston terrier. She named him Phiz. Helen owned many dogs during her lifetime, but Phiz was one of her favorites.

In spite of this show of friendship, college was often a lonely place for Helen. When students

Helen and Phiz, the Boston terrier that she received as a gift from her fellow students at Radcliffe University.

passed her in hallways, they gave no sign of greeting. It was the same when she entered a crowded lecture room. This saddened Helen. "In the classroom, I am practically alone," she said.

It was the same with the teachers. Most of them she found to be "impersonal." She later remarked, "the professor is as remote [from me] as if he were talking through a telephone."

Helen still managed to get excellent grades at Radcliffe. One of her teachers praised her for the compositions that she wrote. He suggested that she write about herself. He wanted her to tell about the unusual world in which she lived.

The teacher showed what Helen had written to an editor of a popular magazine for women. The editor was very impressed. He asked Helen to write a series of articles for the magazine. In the articles, she would tell the story of her life.

The editor told her she would be paid three thousand dollars for the articles. Helen was thrilled. At the time, three thousand dollars was as much as the average American earned in an entire year.

Helen agreed to write the articles. She and Annie asked twenty-five-year-old John Macy to help them. Macy was an instructor at Harvard. He immediately learned the manual alphabet so that he could "talk" with Helen.

As Macy worked with Helen, he marveled at her

astounding memory. He said, "She remembered whole passages, some of which she had not seen for many weeks. . . ."

After Helen's articles had appeared in the magazine, they were used in a book. The book was published in 1903. At the time, Helen was in her third year at Radcliffe. The book was titled *The Story of My Life*.

Helen dedicated the book to Alexander Graham Bell. She praised him as the man "who has taught the deaf to speak and enabled the listening ear to hear speech from the Atlantic to the Rockies."

Newspapers of the time praised *The Story of My Life*. "It seems to be the style of a practiced writer rather than a college girl," said the *San Francisco Chronicle*. *The Literary Digest* applauded the book because it was the story of someone who enjoyed life and did not feel sorry for herself.

The Story of My Life became a remarkable success. In 1996, it was named one of the most important books of the twentieth century by the New York Public Library.

An honor student, Helen graduated from Radcliffe College in 1904.

The year after *The Story of My Life* was published, Helen graduated from college. She was one of ninety-six young women who received their degrees from Radcliffe that year.

When her name was called out, Helen rose from

her seat and moved toward the platform and the Radcliffe president. Every eye was on her as she mounted the steps, using Annie's arm as a guide. As she approached the president, she put out her hand to receive her diploma. The audience raised the roof with applause and cheers. On Helen's diploma the Latin words *cum laude* had been added, which meant "with honors."

"College has breathed new life into my mind and given me new views of things..." Helen said. "I grow stronger in the conviction that there is nothing good or right which we cannot accomplish if we have the will to strive."

In later years, however, Helen revealed that college had left her somewhat saddened. Radcliffe, Helen pointed out, had failed to take notice of all that Annie had done during her years there.

"Together we went through Radcliffe College," Helen wrote. "Day after day during four years, she sat beside me in lecture halls and spelled into my hand word by word what the professors had said; and nearly all the books she read to me in the same way.

"Yet when I received my degree from Radcliffe, not a word of recognition was given her!" That "thoughtlessness," said Helen, became "a thorn in my memory."

WRITER, SPEAKER, TRAVELER

"OUR CHIEF HAPPINESS IS THAT WE have a real home of our own. It is old-fashioned, roomy, and cheerful. I never had a room for my books before."

That is how Helen described the farmhouse that she and Annie purchased in Wrentham, Massachusetts, south of Boston. They moved in just before Helen graduated from Radcliffe.

Helen was twenty-four years old now. She knew she must decide what she would do with the rest of her life. She was unsure what profession to choose. One thing was certain, however. She knew that she would "devote [her] life to those who suffer from loss of sight."

Helen kept busy writing. She wrote one magazine article after another. Her articles were about people who were blind and the special problems they faced.

John Macy often visited Helen and Annie in their Wrentham home. He helped Helen with her writing.

Annie's eyesight continued to get worse. But John was always there to help. "I do not know what we should do without John," Helen said in a letter to a friend.

John was becoming more and more important in the lives of Helen and Annie. Helen sensed that Annie and John were falling in love.

Helen was right. John asked Annie to marry him. Annie said no. She explained that she could never let anyone come between her and Helen.

John promised her that Helen would come first. He said that Helen's life would be just as before.

Even that promise was not enough for Annie. She told John that he must get Helen to approve.

John spoke to Helen in the study of their

Annie Sullivan reads over John Macy's shoulder. Helen is standing at the left.

Wrentham home. He told her that he had asked Annie to marry him.

"Do you love her?" Helen asked, tapping the words into John's hand.

With a quick hand signal, John said yes.

"Does she love you?"

Another hand signal. Another yes.

"Then marry her, of course," Helen declared.

John and Annie were married in 1905. The couple settled down in the Wrentham house with Helen.

Helen continued to write. John assisted her. With his help, Helen finished another book. Titled *The World I Live In*, the book was published in 1908.

The book was a big success. In it, Helen explained how she used her sense of touch to appreciate "the delicate shapes of flowers, the noble forms of trees, and the range of mighty winds."

Vibrations were very important in Helen's life. "I derive much knowledge of everyday matters from the jars and jolts which are to be felt everywhere in the house.

"It is impossible to mistake a child's patter for the tread of a grown person . . . I know when one kneels, kicks, shakes something, sits down, or gets up."

Knowing that the public was curious about her world, Helen decided to try giving lectures. She first took special lessons to strengthen her vocal cords. Otherwise, she knew she would not be able to be heard in a lecture hall.

Helen was able to use her sense of touch to learn about nature.

By listening to an instrument's vibrations, Helen was able to enjoy music. She could not tell one song from another, however.

Helen faced her first audience in Montclair, New Jersey, in 1913. Her lecture was titled: "The Heart and the Hand in the Right Use of Our Senses." Annie was at her side.

As she began to speak, Helen felt the grip of panic. But she kept going. Stage fright finally overcame her. She left the stage in tears.

Helen thought she had been a dismal failure. She

was wrong. The audience loved her performance. Cheers and applause rang out.

In time, Helen became one of America's most popular speakers. She and Annie developed a plan for their appearances. Annie would speak first, explaining the methods that she had used in teaching Helen to read, write, and communicate. Then she would introduce Helen. They would demonstrate how Helen was able to read lips with her fingers. Then Helen spoke directly to the audience. Annie would repeat each sentence.

Helen once spoke at a conference of doctors at the Harvard Medical School. Afterward, a reporter asked her whether she knew that she had spoken before a large crowd.

"I should say I did," Helen replied. "I could feel them and smell them."

"How did you feel them?" the reporter asked.

"By any number of vibrations through the air, and through the floor, from the moving of feet or the scraping of chairs and by the warmth when there are people around."

"How could you tell by your sense of smell?"

"There was a doctor's odor," Helen answered.

"Do you mean to say that doctors have a special odor which you can recognize?"

"A very decided odor," Helen said. "It's partly the smell of ether and partly the smell that lingers from the sick rooms in which they have been. But I can tell many professions from their odor."

"Which ones?"

"Doctors, painters, sculptors, masons, carpenters, druggists, and cooks."

"What does the carpenter smell like, and the druggist?

"The carpenter is always accompanied by the odor of wood. The druggist is saturated with various drugs. There is a painter who comes here often and I can tell the minute he comes anywhere near me."

"Could you tell my work in that way?" the reporter asked. "Do you smell any ink?"

"No, a typewriter, I think," Helen said with a grin.

"Could you *really* tell that?" the reporter asked.

Helen laughed. "I'm afraid that was a guess," she said.

The next year, 1914, Helen, Annie, and Helen's mother set out on a lecture tour that took them to the West Coast. The lectures drew enthusiastic crowds.

In 1915, they planned to repeat the tour. Helen wrote to her mother about it: "...We start for the Middle West the second week in January, go through Ohio, Indiana, Iowa, Kansas, St. Louis, down to Texas as far as El Paso, then to Lower California, and up to San Francisco and back home through California. It will be most interesting for you I'm sure; do come."

In preparing for the trip, Helen and Annie hired an assistant. She was twenty-four-year-old Polly Thomson. Newly arrived from Scotland, Polly wanted to settle in the United States.

Polly did not know the manual alphabet. She could not read braille. She had never heard of Helen Keller. But she was bright and quick. She soon became valuable as a secretary and household

Polly Thomson (left) became Helen's secretary and assistant in 1914. Here she gives Helen a dancing lesson.

manager. "She seems to know what I want without my telling her," Helen said of Polly in a letter to her sister. Later, when Annie became ill, Polly would take over Annie's role as Helen's constant companion.

CHAPTER 10

A MARRIAGE
OFFER

THROUGHOUT HER LIFE, HELEN DID not hesitate to let people know what was on her mind. When World War I broke out in Europe in 1914, Helen had an opinion. She did not want the United States to get involved in the fighting.

"I look upon the world as my fatherland," she wrote, "and every war has for me the horror of a family feud. I hold true patriotism to be the brotherhood and mutual service of all men."

Public opinion in the United States supported the war, however. Helen's antiwar views caused her popularity to shrink. Fewer people were interested in hearing her speak. Helen's lecture tour in 1916 was a failure.

When Helen and Annie returned to their home in Wrentham, Massachusetts, there was more bad news. A doctor found Annie to be seriously ill. Her illness was made worse by her marriage to John Macy, which had become troubled. Annie and John eventually separated.

A doctor ordered Annie to spend time at a health resort. It was decided that Polly would go along to help nurse Annie back to health.

Helen invited her mother to come to Wrentham. There was also a third member of the household. His name was Peter Fagan. He was twenty-nine years old. Helen and Annie had hired Peter as a secretary.

Peter taught himself braille and the manual alphabet. Helen enjoyed the young man's company. He had a good sense of humor. They soon found that they shared the same views on the war and social issues of the day.

One September evening in 1916, while Helen was sitting alone in her study, Peter entered the room. "For a long time," she wrote, "he held my hand in silence, then he began talking to me tenderly. I was surprised that he cared so much about me.

"He was full of plans for my happiness. He said if I would marry him, he would always be near to help me in the difficulties of life.

"The sweetness of being loved enchanted me," Helen wrote. Her hand trembling, she signaled to Peter that she would accept his offer of marriage.

Helen was excited. She wanted to tell Annie and her mother right away "about the wonderful thing that happened to me."

But Peter said they should wait. He knew that Helen's mother did not like him. He felt certain that she would disapprove of the marriage.

"Let us keep our love secret a little while," Peter said. "Your teacher is too ill to be excited just now and we must tell her first."

Helen didn't like the idea of keeping their plan a secret. She wrote, "The thought of not sharing my happiness with my mother [and Annie]...little by little destroyed the joy of being loved."

The couple moved ahead with their plans. They

Annie Sullivan "speaks" to Helen as Helen's mother looks on.

traveled to Boston together. At the registrar's office there, they sought a marriage license.

Then a Boston newspaper reporter found out about the couple's request for a marriage license. The Boston newspapers were soon filled with stories about Helen's romance.

Helen's mother was furious. She went to Helen's room. She picked up Helen's hand. Helen knew immediately something was wrong.

"The papers are full of a dreadful story about you and him," were the words she tapped into Helen's hand. "What does it all mean? Tell me!"

Helen pretended not to know what her mother was talking about.

Her mother continued. "Are you engaged to him? Did you apply for a marriage license?"

Helen denied everything.

At the time, Helen was thirty-six years old. She was famous throughout the world. But to Mrs. Keller, Helen was simply a daughter who had acted foolishly.

Mrs. Keller ordered Peter out of the house. She wouldn't even let him say good-bye to Helen. Then she announced that they would be returning to the family home in Tuscumbia.

Peter followed them to Alabama. One night he showed up on the front porch of the Keller home. Mrs. Keller had him sent away.

Peter and Helen eventually realized that there would be no marriage. Peter withdrew from Helen's life.

Years later, Helen wrote of the romance. "The brief love will remain in my life," she said, "a little island of joy surrounded by dark waters."

CHAPTER 11

ON STAGE

BY THE EARLY MONTHS OF 1917, Annie Sullivan's health had improved. She and Polly Thomson returned to the Wrentham home to be reunited with Helen.

The terrible war that Helen had feared had become a reality. During April of 1917, the United States declared war on Germany. "All happiness has left us with the departure of peace from our land," Helen wrote.

The war wasn't Helen's only concern. Money had become a problem for Helen and Annie. The lecture business was producing little income. No longer were they earning enough to support themselves.

The house in Massachusetts was a big expense. Helen and Annie decided to sell it.

It saddened Helen to be leaving Wrentham. She had lived there for thirteen years. "I shall always think of it as my home," she said. Helen, Annie, and Polly Thomson moved from Wrentham into a smaller house in the Forest Hills section of New York City's borough of Queens.

The next year brought news that promised to end their financial problems. A Hollywood producer wanted to make a film based on Helen's life. The idea excited Helen. In the spring of 1918, Helen, Annie, Polly Thomson, and Helen's mother set out for Hollywood.

They arrived to find the movie business booming. It was, however, the time of silent films. It would be several more years before sound was added to film and "talkies" became popular. Because movies had no sound, the fact that Helen was not able to speak well was not a problem.

In Hollywood, Helen and Annie met many of the most famous movie stars of the time. Their favorite was Charlie Chaplin. He had earned worldwide fame for his ability to make people laugh. Helen and Charlie Chaplin seemed to understand each other. The two became good friends.

The movie about Helen's life was called *Deliverance*. After the cameras started filming, Helen was called upon to read braille and act as if

While in Hollywood, Helen (center) became friends with comedian Charlie Chaplin. With them are Polly Thomson (left) and Annie Sullivan (right).

she was answering her mail. She was also asked to play a trumpet, ride a frisky horse, and take a ride in a small, open cockpit airplane.

The airplane flight thrilled her. She wrote: "Was I afraid? How could fear hold back my spirit, long accustomed to soar? Up, up, up the machine bore me until I lost the odors of flying dust...."

When *Deliverance* opened at movie theaters in August of 1918, it was highly praised. To *The New York Times*, it was "one of the triumphs of the motion picture."

But it did not appeal to the public. Few people went to see the movie and *Deliverance* was a financial failure. Helen came out of the experience poorer than she went into it.

Back home, Helen and Annie sought another way to earn money. At the time, popular entertainment in the United States included vaudeville. In a typical vaudeville program, dancers, singers, comedians, acrobats, and even trained animals were presented on stage as separate acts.

Helen and Annie decided to prepare a vaudeville

act. Many of Helen's friends were shocked that she would even consider becoming a vaudeville performer. They had a low opinion of vaudeville. They said it appealed only to the "lower classes."

Helen shrugged off their comments. She and Annie went to work to produce what Helen called a "dignified act."

Helen's career in vaudeville began in February 1920. It was a great success from the very beginning.

The act lasted about twenty minutes. It began with the theater curtain rising to show a homey room with a fireplace. At one side of the room stood a piano on which rested a vase of fresh roses.

Annie Sullivan, wearing a long gown, walked out onto the stage and into the spotlight. When the applause died down, she talked for several minutes about Helen's life.

As soon as Annie had finished, a pair of curtains at the rear of the stage opened. Helen walked out. Guided by the scent of the roses, she made her way to the piano. As she neared the piano, she reached out and touched it.

Annie took Helen by the arm and guided her to the center of the stage. Then Helen would speak briefly to the audience. The words came slowly. Each one was a struggle. Men and women sat on the edges of their seats, leaning forward, as they tried to understand what she was saying. They were in awe.

"What I have to say is very simple," Helen began. "My teacher has told you how a word from her hand touched the darkness of my mind and I awoke to the gladness of life. I was dumb; now I speak. I owe this to the hands and hearts of others. Through their love I found my soul and God and happiness."

The performance ended with Helen taking questions from the audience. Some of the more popular questions, along with Helen's answers, included the following:

Do you close your eyes when you sleep?
I guess I do, but I never stayed awake to see.

Who are the most unhappy people?
People who have nothing to do.

Helen puts on stage makeup before one of her vaudeville appearances.

Do you think women should hold office?
Yes, if they can get enough of their fellow
citizens to vote for them.

What brings you the greatest satisfaction?
Work, accomplishment.

Who are your best pals?
Books.

Helen loved being on stage. She loved the excitement of the theater and what she called the "life vibrations" of the audience.

"I found the world of vaudeville much more amusing than the world I had always lived in, and I liked it," she later wrote. "I liked to feel the warm tide of human life...pulsing around me."

It was not just the excitement of the theater that caused Helen to like vaudeville. Her act with Annie put an end to their financial problems. Helen and Annie were among vaudeville's highest-paid performers. At some theaters, they earned as much as $2,000 a week.

Helen and Annie continued in vaudeville for five years. The two women were on tour in Los Angeles in 1921 when Annie tapped sad news into Helen's hand. Helen's mother had died suddenly in Alabama.

But the death of her mother did not stop Helen

from going on stage that night. "Every fiber of my being cried out at the thought of facing the audience," Helen wrote later. "But it had to be done."

Helen suffered more misfortune the next year. While she and Annie were presenting their act in Toronto, Canada, Annie was struck down with the flu. Polly Thomson had to take over for her.

When she got well, Annie returned to the stage. But she later lost her voice. Again, Polly replaced her.

"Polly and I go on the stage twice a day," Helen wrote. "She tells how Miss Sullivan taught me, and then I answer questions and give my message as usual."

Polly proved to be a first-rate substitute for Annie. But Helen was quick to admit that she felt lost without Annie at her side.

CHAPTER 12

CRUSADER

H ELEN WAS IN HER MID-FORTIES now. She could look back on a life filled with achievement. She had been a writer, a public speaker, a movie actress, and a vaudeville performer. Now she was ready to take on a new career.

Helen had always worked on behalf of persons who were blind and deaf-blind. But beginning in 1924, Helen began to play a more active role in her work for the physically challenged. She became a staff member of the American Foundation for the Blind. From that year until her death, she was active with the organization.

Helen had a special talent for fund-raising. Her name was like magic. She and Annie began to tour the country to collect money for the American Foundation for the Blind. It was hard work. Helen and Annie went before the public several times a week.

Their appearances were similar to those that they had made as vaudeville performers. First, an artist who was blind, usually a violinist or pianist, would play. Annie would then speak, explaining Helen's education. Next, she would introduce Helen, who would make a short speech. Helen would end by asking the people in the audience to donate money for people who were blind.

People crowded lecture halls and other meeting places to hear Helen speak. She was called the "perfect symbol" of the physically challenged. She explained to audiences that "the great need of the blind was not charity but opportunity."

With each appearance, Helen and Annie raised thousands of dollars. One newspaper hailed their efforts with the headline PURSES FLY OPEN TO HELEN KELLER.

Helen and Annie also won the support of some of

Helen Keller at age forty-five in 1925. She began touring the country, raising funds for the American Foundation for the Blind.

the wealthiest people of the day. Henry Ford, the founder of the Ford Motor Company, gave to their cause. So did John D. Rockefeller, one of the most noted business leaders of the time.

In 1926, their fund-raising efforts took Helen and Annie to the White House. President Calvin Coolidge welcomed them.

The President was known to be quiet and unsmiling. With Helen, he quickly relaxed, however. "They say you are cold, but you are not," Helen told him. "You are a dear President."

From the White House, Helen and Annie were driven to the Senate Office Building. There they met Thomas D. Schall, a Minnesota senator who was blind. Senator Schall had just completed a long and difficult election campaign. During the campaign, he had delivered 287 speeches.

"What did you find to say 287 times?" Helen asked him.

"Oh, I just said the same things over," the senator replied.

"That's just what I'd do, too," Helen said with a grin.

In their work for the American Foundation for the Blind, Helen and Annie visited 123 cities in the

Helen poses with a smiling President Calvin Coolidge on a winter day in 1926.

United States. They spoke to more than a quarter of a million people. They raised more than $1 million in donations, a huge amount for the time.

Beginning in 1927, Helen spent most of her time writing. Her chief project was *Midstream: My Later*

Life. The book was published in 1929. It was a success from the first day it appeared in bookstores.

After *Midstream* was published, Helen, Annie, and Polly Thomson traveled to Europe. One reason for the journey was Annie's failing eyesight. Helen wanted Annie to experience the world before she lost her ability to see. While in Europe, Helen celebrated her fiftieth birthday.

When they returned to the United States, Helen and Polly went to work again for the American Foundation for the Blind. But now when they traveled to raise funds, Annie stayed behind. She was too ill to make long journeys.

Annie's eyesight was almost completely gone. She could see only shadows. She also had heart disease. In the spring of 1935, she entered a hospital for treatment.

The next spring, Annie had an operation in an effort to improve her eyesight. The operation weakened her. Annie's health continued to fail.

Annie Sullivan died on October 15, 1936. Helen was at her bedside, holding her hand.

Helen and Annie had been companions for almost fifty years. "The light, the music, and the glory of life had been withdrawn," Helen wrote.

Later that year, Helen and Polly Thomson traveled to England and Scotland. They planned to visit Polly's family in Scotland.

Now it was Polly who was at Helen's side. Often the two women would walk the decks of the ocean liner together. Polly would take Helen's hand and describe the blue sea and the seagulls circling the ship.

Returning to her home was very difficult for Helen. She missed Annie terribly. As she walked through the rooms of the house, she reached out to feel Annie's desk. She felt the chair on which Annie had sat. When Helen touched Annie's books, she was all but overcome by a wave of sadness.

"I had watched the darkness descending upon the eyes she had used during half a century to assist me and enrich my happiness," Helen wrote. "Only by the hardest work could I shut out that mournful memory and the heart-stabbing loneliness that pursued my every moment."

CHAPTER 13

DARING ADVENTURE

MANY OF HELEN'S FRIENDS THOUGHT that Annie Sullivan's death might put an end to the active life that Helen had always led. How could Helen possibly manage without her?

There would be no more lecture tours, they thought. No more travel. They believed that Helen might return to the family home in Tuscumbia, Alabama. There she would lead a quiet life with her sister.

Helen's friends were wrong.

"Life is daring adventure or nothing," Helen once wrote. After Annie's death, Helen's life changed little. She was to live thirty-two more years after Annie died. And her life continued to be one of "daring adventure."

When the Japanese government asked Helen to come to Japan to raise money for people who were blind and deaf, Helen said yes. She and Polly Thomson left by ocean liner for Japan in April 1937. It was the first of many world tours for the two women.

Helen was already famous in Japan. When she arrived, a cheering crowd greeted her. The crowd included several thousand school children. They waved Japanese and American flags.

Helen gave ninety-seven lectures in Japan. She spoke in thirty-nine cities. Mobs of photographers and newspaper reporters followed her everywhere.

In her speeches, Helen talked about the ways in which people who were blind might help themselves. She also spoke of her hopes for world peace.

Not long after her return to the United States, Helen and Polly sold the house in Forest Hills. It held too many sad memories for them.

Helen Keller (center) made several visits to Japan, becoming a favorite of the Japanese people. On one of her trips, wearing a loose, wide-sleeved Japanese robe, she posed with Polly Thomson and a trio of Japanese friends.

"I can never, never get used to this house without Teacher [Annie]," Helen once admitted to Polly.

"Nor can I," Polly replied.

Helen and Polly moved to Easton, Connecticut. Their new house was a gift from the American Foundation for the Blind. Helen called it Arcan Ridge.

"We never loved a place more than Arcan Ridge," Helen later wrote. "It is a...house surrounded by meadows, woods, brooks, and the old New England stone walls....I am especially delighted with my study which has spacious bookshelves...." Helen would live at Arcan Ridge for the rest of her life.

During the summer months, Helen would awaken very early. By five o'clock, she was at work in her flower garden. She was able to tell the flowers from the weeds by her sense of touch.

She also picked blueberries. Her sensitive fingers told her which ones were ripe. She liked to cut grass and rake leaves, too.

At Arcan Ridge, Helen could take a bath alone. She could pick out the clothes that she wanted to wear, and dress herself.

A bell was rung to announce mealtime. If she was outside or moving about the house, she could not sense it. But if she was working at her desk, she could feel the bell's vibrations. She would answer the bell by pounding on the floor.

After she had settled in the new house, Helen

Arcan Ridge, Helen's home in Easton, Connecticut. Railings (in foreground) helped her make her way about the property by herself.

began writing a book about the life of Annie Sullivan. She spent every possible moment working on it, but it would be many years before the book would be finished.

Late in 1941, when she was busy with the book about Annie, Helen received shocking news. The Japanese had bombed the American naval base at Pearl Harbor, Hawaii. The next day the United States entered World War II.

Helen had always felt close to the Japanese people. She was deeply saddened by the attack on Pearl Harbor. Yet, she wanted to do whatever she could to help the United States in the war effort.

She soon found an important role to play. She began visiting soldiers who were wounded or blind in military hospitals. The young men were often surprised to meet her. To many of them, Helen Keller was a great person. They had read about her in school or heard about her from their parents.

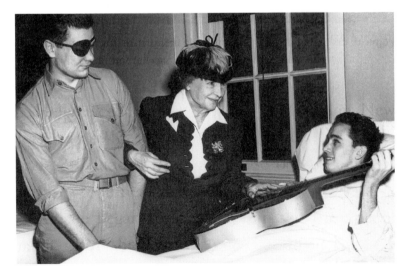

During World War II, Helen made frequent visits to the wounded in U.S. military hospitals.

Helen would hold the hands of the soldiers. Sometime she would stroke their hair. Polly would speak the words that Helen tapped into her hand. Helen never failed to be bright and cheerful during her hospital visits. She always carried a message of hope. Helen called her work with the wounded soldiers "the crowning experience of my life."

Eleanor Roosevelt, the wife of President Franklin D. Roosevelt, wrote about Helen and her work. She praised Helen for the healing power of her visits.

After World War II ended in 1945, Helen continued her travel on behalf of people who were blind and deaf-blind. She made nine worldwide tours. These took her to thirty-four different countries.

Many nations of the world honored Helen for her work. She received the Sacred Treasure Award from Japan and the Legion of Honor from France. She also received Brazil's Southern Cross and the Philippines' Golden Heart.

During her lifetime, Helen met every American

When Helen asked to "see" the face of President Dwight D. Eisenhower, he responded with his famous grin.

president from Grover Cleveland to John F. Kennedy. In October of 1953, she visited the White House to meet President Dwight D. Eisenhower.

The President was at his desk when Helen and Polly Thomson arrived. He got up and walked toward them. A smile crossed his face.

"It's so nice to see you," the president said. "It is wonderful of you to come down here."

"I am proud to meet you, Mr. President," Helen replied.

Then Helen asked, "Mr. President, may I touch your face? I want to put my hand on your face and see your celebrated smile."

The President said yes.

Helen went over the President's face carefully. Then she said, "You have a wonderful smile."

Then the President grinned. "But not much hair," he said.

TO ANOTHER ROOM

LATE IN 1958, HELEN'S LIFE TURNED sad again. Polly Thomson became seriously ill. She died in 1960 at the age of seventy-six. She had been Helen's companion for more than half of her life.

Once again, Helen was alone. Then Winnie Corbally, who had nursed Polly in her final days, became Helen's new companion. Winnie was skilled at spelling into Helen's hand.

Helen celebrated her eightieth birthday on June 27, 1960. Her life of daring adventure was coming to a close.

Yet Helen continued to be bright and positive. "I believe that all through these dark and silent years God has been using my life for a purpose I do not know," she said. "But one day I shall understand, and then I will be satisfied."

Helen's name was in the news again in 1962. A popular movie called *The Miracle Worker* presented the story of Helen's early life.

Originally, *The Miracle Worker* had been presented as a television drama. Then it was performed on stage in New York City. One newspaper called it a "smash hit." The play ran for almost two years.

In both the play and the movie, actress Patty Duke played the part of Helen as a seven year old. Anne Bancroft was Annie Sullivan. Both actresses were highly praised. Both won Academy Awards for their performances in the film.

Thirteen-year-old Patty Duke paid a visit to Helen at Arcan Ridge. After they were introduced, Helen gave the child actress a beautiful Japanese doll from her collection.

The two went for a walk in the gardens that Helen loved. To guide Helen, railings had been put up along the walkways.

Helen greets Patty Duke, who portrayed her in The Miracle Worker.
The young actress won an Academy Award for her performance.

"To understand me," Patty Duke recalled, she would put her thumb on my lips and her fingers on different vibration points. She didn't miss a thing.

"She told me the name of every tree and bush and flower."

Patty Duke remembered that Helen had thin white hair. It was "almost like an angel's hair," she said, "and [she had] a terrific smile.

"And she was so jolly," said the young actress, "like a jolly grandmother. I had expected serious and sweet, but not jolly, not someone who loved to laugh."

During the final years of her life, Helen was frail and had little energy. Most of her days were spent in a wheelchair or her bed.

Helen's fingers were not as sensitive as they once had been. She had to warm them before she could read braille. One of her great pleasures was to have Winnie read to her.

In 1964, Helen received a special tribute. President Lyndon Johnson awarded her the Presidential Medal of Freedom. The medal is the nation's highest honor.

Late in May 1968, Helen suffered a heart attack. A few days later, on June 1, 1968, Helen died.

Winnie Corbally was at her bedside. "She died gently," Winnie said.

Helen's ashes were taken to the National Cathedral in Washington. There they were placed

A choir made up of students from the Perkins School for the Blind enters the Washington National Cathedral for Helen's funeral services.

next to the ashes of Annie Sullivan and Polly Thomson.

When Helen was in her seventies, a friend had asked her, "Do you believe in life after death?"

"Most certainly," Helen declared. "It is no more than passing from one room to another."

Then, speaking slowly, Helen added, "But there's a difference for me, you know. Because in that other —room—I will be able to see."

CHAPTER 15

HELEN KELLER REMEMBERED

In June of each year, Tuscumbia, Alabama, becomes a busy place. Thousands of visitors pour into the small town in northwestern Alabama where Helen Keller was born. They travel there for the Helen Keller Festival. The event honors the memory of Helen Keller's life and work.

There's a parade through downtown. There's an arts and crafts show. Tour guides lead visitors to Helen Keller's birthplace and other historic sites.

On weekends during the festival, *The Miracle Worker* is performed outdoors. Audiences watch in awe as the play about Helen's early life unfolds.

Helen Keller could not see. She could not hear. Yet she led an active life. She wrote books and magazine articles. She gave lectures. She traveled the world. She became one of the most admired women in America.

People throughout the world remain interested in Helen Keller. They want to know more about her.

In 1999, *Time Magazine* named Helen Keller one of the one hundred most influential people of the

Helen Keller's writing is an inspiration for people all over the world.

twentieth century. The magazine called her the "champion of the blind."

Helen Keller's life story inspires people. It makes them want to do well in their own lives. Helen Keller was able to rise above her physical challenges. But that is only part of her story.

She devoted much of her life to helping other people who were blind and deaf-blind. On her eightieth birthday, she told a newspaper reporter, "I will always—as long as I have breath—work for the handicapped."

Helen not only raised money for people with disabilities, she also sought to improve their living and working conditions.

At the time Helen Keller was growing up, people who were blind were treated poorly. They were often kept in buildings called "asylums."

Helen Keller and the work she did helped change conditions for people who are blind and others who face physical challenges. Today, the government and many private organizations are available to help people who are blind and deaf-blind.

The American Foundation for the Blind is one of the leaders in the field. The organization works with government officials and private companies in seeking to improve the lives of people who are blind. It publishes books and pamphlets about blindness. It records "Talking Books" for people who cannot see well enough to read.

Several organizations that help people who are blind bear Helen Keller's name.

HELEN KELLER
ANNE SULLIVAN

A portrait of Helen and Annie Sullivan, which dates to 1898, served as the basis of a U.S. postage stamp that was issued in 1980.

The Helen Keller National Center for Deaf-Blind Youths and Adults, through its training programs, helps people who are deaf-blind to become active in their homes and communities. In June each year, the organization sponsors the Helen Keller Deaf-Blind Awareness Week.

Helen Keller Services for the Blind is an

In Bangladesh, a representative of Helen Keller Worldwide gives out Vitamin A capsules to young children. Vitamin A helps to prevent blindness.

organization that is active in job training. It seeks to help people who are blind lead independent lives.

Helen Keller Worldwide works internationally. The organization assists nations in Europe, Asia, and the Americas in preventing or curing eye diseases. Helen Keller Worldwide is active in eighteen different countries.

Helen Keller has not been forgotten. She is a

symbol of hope and courage for people in every country of the world.

At the funeral services for Helen Keller in 1968, Senator Lister Hill of Alabama spoke of her. He said, "She will live on, one of the few, the immortal names not born to die. Her spirit will endure as long as man can read and stories can be told of the woman who showed the world there are no boundaries to courage and faith."

CHRONOLOGY

1880 (June 27) Helen Keller born in Tuscumbia, Alabama.

1882 Keller loses sight, hearing, and power of speech.

1887 Anne Sullivan arrives in Tuscumbia to teach Helen.

1888 Keller visits Perkins Institution for the Blind in Boston.

1894 Keller enters Wright-Humason School in New York City.

1896 Keller enters Cambridge School for Young Ladies.

1900 Keller enters Radcliffe College.

1903 Keller writes and publishes *The Story of My Life*.

1904 Keller graduates from Radcliffe College.

1905 Anne Sullivan marries John Macy.

1908 Keller writes and publishes *The World I Live In*.

1913 Keller writes and publishes *Out of the Dark*.

1914 Keller hires Polly Thomson.

1916 Keller takes out marriage license with Peter Fagan.

1918 Keller stars in film *Deliverance*.

1920 Keller begins career in vaudeville with Sullivan.

1924 Keller begins work for the American Foundation for the Blind.

1927 Keller writes and publishes *My Religion*.

1929 Keller writes and publishes *Midstream*.

1936   Anne Sullivan Macy dies.

1937   Keller tours Japan with Thomson.

1938   Keller writes and publishes *Journal*.

1955   Keller writes and publishes *Teacher: Anne Sullivan Macy*.

1960   Polly Thomson dies.

1968   (June 1) Helen Keller dies at her Easton, Connecticut home.

BIBLIOGRAPHY

Primary Sources

Keller, Helen. *Journal*. New York: Doubleday, Doran, 1938.

———. *Midstream: My Later Life*. New York: Doubleday, Doran, 1929.

———. *My Religion*. New York: Doubleday, Doran, 1927.

———. *Out of the Dark*. New York: Doubleday, Page, 1913.

———. *The Story of My Life*. New York: Signet Classics, 1988.

———. *Teacher: Anne Sullivan Macy*. New York: Doubleday, 1955.

———. *The World I Live In*. New York: Century, 1908.

Secondary Sources

Herrmann, Dorothy. *Helen Keller, A Life*. New York: Alfred A. Knopf, 1998.

Lash, Joseph P. *Helen and Teacher; The Story of Helen Keller and Anne Sullivan Macy*. New York: Addison-Wesley, 1997.

FURTHER READING

Davidson, Margaret. *Helen Keller*. New York: Scholastic, 1997.

———. *Helen Keller's Teacher*. New York: Scholastic, 1992.

Graff, Stewart. *Helen Keller*. New York: Dell, 1991.

Nicholson, Lois P. *Helen Keller, Humanitarian*. New York, Chelsea House, 1996.

FOR MORE INFORMATION

American Foundation for the Blind
Makes available a booklet titled, "Helen Keller"; also, a printed card with raised dots to instruct one in the use of the braille alphabet and numbers.
11 Penn Plaza
New York, New York 10001
Phone: (212) 502-7600; (800) 232-5463
Website: www.afb.org

Perkins School for the Blind
Makes available copies of articles about Helen Keller.
175 North Beacon St.
Watertown, Massachusetts 02172
Phone: (617) 924-3434

Helen Keller National Center for Deaf-Blind Youths and Adults
Write for copies of brochures titled "Facts about Deaf Blindness" and "Guidelines for Helping Deaf-Blind Persons."
111 Middle Neck Road
Sands Point, New York 11050
Phone: (516) 944-8900
Website: www.helenkeller.org/national

Ivy Green/Birthplace of Helen Keller
Write for color brochure describing Ivy Green, Helen Keller's birthplace.
300 West North Commons
Tuscumbia, Alabama 35674
Phone: (205) 383-4066
Website: www.bham.net/Keller/home.html

PHOTO CREDITS

INDEX

Bold numbers refer to photographs